HALLOWEEN
fun and food

Sara Lewis

hamlyn

First published in 2002
by Hamlyn a division of
Octopus Publishing Group Limited
2–4 Heron Quays, London E14 4JP

ISBN 0 600 60711 9

Printed and bound in China
10 9 8 7 6 5 4 3 2 1

Notes

1 Standard level spoon measurements
are used in all recipes.
1 tablespoon = one 15 ml spoon
1 teaspoon = one 5 ml spoon

2 Both metric and imperial
measurements are given for the
recipes. Use one set of measurements
only, not a mixture of both.

3 Eggs should be medium unless
otherwise stated. The Department of
Health advises that eggs should not be
consumed raw. This book contains
some dishes made with lightly cooked
eggs. It is prudent for more vulnerable
people, such as pregnant and nursing
mothers, invalids, the elderly, babies
and young children, to avoid dishes
made with lightly cooked eggs. Use
dried egg white or pasteurized whole
eggs as an alternative. Once prepared,
these dishes should be kept
refrigerated and used promptly.

4 Fresh herbs should be used unless
otherwise stated. If unavailable, use
dried herbs as an alternative but halve
the quantities stated.

5 Ovens should be preheated to
the specified temperature. If using
a fan-assisted oven, follow the
manufacturer's instructions for
adjusting the time and temperature.
Grills should also be preheated.

6 This book includes dishes made with
nuts and nut derivatives. It is advisable
for readers with known allergic
reactions to nuts and nut derivatives
and those who may be potentially
vulnerable to these allergies, such as
pregnant and nursing mothers, invalids,
the elderly, babies and children, to avoid
dishes made with nuts and nut oils. It is
also prudent to check the labels of pre-
prepared ingredients for the possible
inclusion of nut derivatives.

7 Pumpkin weight specified in recipes is
the prepared weight – after the skin
and seeds have been removed.

☆ **SAFETY NOTE**
Never leave burning candles or
pumpkin lanterns unattended or allow
children to use them without adult
supervision.

Contents

Introduction

Whatever you're doing this Halloween, this book can help you. Whether you're planning a quiet evening with the family, throwing a noisy children's party or having a celebration with friends, you will find a wealth of original ways to decorate your home, ideas for devilishly good food to share, plus fun-filled games for all ages to make it a night to remember.

FROM KIDS TO ADULTS

Halloween provides an ideal opportunity for a themed children's party. Kids love to dress up, and the more spooky or ghoulish the effect the better. Costumes can be dark and spooky or bright and twinkly and it can be fun to wear masks or use face paints. This book contains suggestions for suitably scary food such as Spider Web Pizzas and grisly Black Cat Jelly set in a carved watermelon. For entertainment choose from traditional favourites such as apple bobbing, or try something new such as the Wizard's Shopping List.

For an adult dinner party, there are suggestions for more sophisticated food such as Honey-Glazed Pork followed by Watermelon and Tequila Granita. While for something a little less formal, there's Bean Pot Supper – a warming dish that will happily sit in the oven until you are ready to dish up. Even if you are not giving a full-scale party you can make an everyday supper into a Halloween celebration by setting the table with some special homemade decorations.

HOW IT ALL BEGAN

In pre-Roman Britain and Ireland the end of summer was marked by a festival at the end of October. It was believed that as evening approached on this day, all those who had died in the past year would come back as spirits in search of living bodies to inhabit for the following year. To ward off these spirits, all fires would be extinguished to make the homes cold and uninviting for the spirits. People also dressed up in ghoulish costumes to try to fool the spirits. As dawn rose, marking the beginning of the new year, the fire festival known as Samhain would be celebrated with torches lit from one central fire and taken to relight fires at home.

THE ROMANS AND CHRISTIANITY When the Romans conquered Britain, they brought with them two festivals of their own, which became combined with the ancient Samhain. The first was Feralia, in late October, when the Romans marked the passing of the dead. The second was a day to honour Pomona, the Roman goddess of fruit and trees. The symbol of Pomona is the apple and the incorporation of this into Samhain probably explains the tradition of 'apple bobbing' often practised today at Halloween.

As Christianity later spread throughout Britain, the festival was adapted to celebrate the night before All Saint's Day (1 November), also known as Allhallow's Eve or Halloween. The traditions of Halloween were brought to North America in the 1840s by the Irish migrants.

WHY DO WE HAVE PUMPKIN LANTERNS?

This custom probably originates with the Irish legend of a notorious drunkard and trickster named Jack. He foolishly tricked the devil into a tree and then trapped him in the

branches by carving the symbol of the cross on the bark of the trunk. Jack struck a deal with the devil that if he promised not to tempt him again, he would let him down from the tree. When Jack died he was denied entrance to heaven because of his evil ways and the devil also refused to let him into hell because of the trick played on him. His one concession was to give Jack a burning ember, which he placed in a hollowed-out turnip as a makeshift lantern to guide him through eternal darkness on earth. Turnip lanterns thus became a traditional feature of Irish Halloween celebrations. When the Irish immigrants settled in America, they found that the large orange pumpkins that grew so plentifully at that time of the year actually made much better lanterns. They were much easier to carve than turnips and, as they were bigger, gave much more light when lit with small, slow burning candles.

Trick or treating

The true origins of this tradition are not known, but it is thought that it is derived from an old Irish practice in which the boys in the village went as a group from house to house, blowing a horn to signal their imminent arrival. The lady of the house would come out and offer money or bread in answer to the sounding of the horn. Failure to supply a treat would usually result in a good-humoured practical joke being played on the householder.

An alternative explanation is that trick or treating derives from an early Christian custom called 'souling' whereby beggars would walk from village to village, begging for soul cakes, made out of bread and currants, in return for saying prayers for the recently deceased to help speed their souls' passage to heaven.

The custom for young children to beg for treats from their neighbours is a much more recent amalgamation of these old traditions and did not really begin until the mid-19th century. While it has always been intended as harmless fun for the children, this tradition has had much bad press. However, if it is done with good humour and sensible ground rules, most neighbourhoods are more than happy to join in the fun.

Harmless tricks

★ Sprinkle flour or icing sugar over the door handle or on the doorstep.
★ Smear the door handle with soft margarine or squirt with aerosol spray string or shaving foam.
★ Wrap paper streamers around the front gate.
★ Pop trick novelties through the letterbox.

Treats to offer

★ Wrapped sweets and toffees
★ Bite-sized chocolate or biscuit bars
★ Candy-covered chocolate sweets
★ Black and orange jelly beans
★ Halloween novelty sweets such as jelly
  fingers or chocolate pumpkins
★ Sugar-free gum
★ Popcorn
★ Small wrapped cheese portions
★ Satsumas
★ Non-edible treats such as pencils, erasers
  or tiny toys

Play it safe

It is wise to follow a few basic guidelines
to keep trick or treating safe and fun for
all concerned:

★ Work out a route with the children and
  telephone your neighbours and friends
  in advance to warn them of a visit, with an
  approximate idea of time.
★ Only go to houses where you are known
  and/or expected.
★ Groups of children should always be
  accompanied by an adult.
★ Explain to the children the importance of
  sticking together.
★ Stress that this is a fun activity and
  shouldn't turn into anything that would
  scare elderly neighbours or those living on
  their own.

Party invites

If you have time, it can be fun to make your own Halloween party invitations. They needn't be over complicated or time-consuming, and can make the party feel much more personalized. Adapt the quantities for the number of invitations you need for your guests.

Spell scroll

YOU WILL NEED
A4 white paper (1 sheet for 2 invites)
red paint or felt-tip pen
black or red ribbon or raffia
plastic spiders or bats
double-sided tape

Cut the sheets of A4 paper in half. Put in the oven and 'cook' at 180°C (350°F), Gas Mark 4, for 7–10 minutes until lightly browned. Singe the edges by burning in a candle or gas flame. Burn very small sections at a time and quickly blow out the flame before it gets too large. Repeat until you have gone all the way round the edge of the paper then cool completely.

Write the party details on each sheet using a fine paintbrush dipped in red paint or a red felt-tip pen. Roll up, and secure the scroll with black or red ribbon or raffia, and splatter with some drops of red paint for blood.

Finish with a black plastic spider or a bat stuck on with double-sided tape, or seal the ribbon or raffia with a little melted candle wax.

Pick up a pumpkin

YOU WILL NEED
corrugated or plain orange card
green pipe cleaners
adhesive tape
black paper
glue stick

For each invite fold a 20 x 10 cm (8 x 4 inch) piece of orange card in half to make a square. With the fold at the top, draw on a pumpkin then cut out, leaving part of the fold uncut to keep the card joined together.

Cut eyes and a mouth out of the front of the card. Add folded pipe cleaners for the pumpkin stalks. Twist the ends together and tuck through the top fold of the card. Secure inside the card with adhesive tape. Cut smaller pumpkins out of black paper and stick inside to write the party details on.

Dancing spooks

For each invite cut a piece of black card 11 x 40 cm (4½ x 16 inch) and fold in half along the longer side. Cut the same number of 11 x 20 cm (4½ x 8 inch) pieces of white paper and on each draw a ghost shape.

Cut out the ghost shapes and then, holding the ghost over the black card so that its head is near the top folded edge, cut the card around the ghost to leave a narrow border of black showing. Leave a section of the fold in the card uncut.

Cut out eye and mouth holes in the paper ghost shapes using small scissors or a craft knife then stick on to the cards using a glue stick. Use a white pen or paint to write the party details inside each card. Alternatively, add a second white ghost shape to the inside of the cards and write the party details in black or red.

Witches' hats

To make three cone shapes for three witches' hats cut a circle 20 cm (8 inches) in diameter from heavy black paper. Cut into three equal segments. Secure the straight edges of each segment together with small strips of adhesive tape.

Cut an 11 cm (4½ inch) diameter circle of black paper for the base of each hat. Pierce the centre and make several 2.5 cm (1 inch) cuts out towards the edge of the circle. Fold up the slits and tape to the inside of the cone.

Add dots of glue to the hat cone and stick on Halloween table confetti or small stars. Tie a length of ribbon around the base of each hat. Write the party details on a small piece of folded coloured card and tuck this inside the ribbon band.

Party decorations

Decorations are essential for creating a Halloween atmosphere. They needn't cost a fortune and can vary from something as simple as black and orange balloons tied with coordinating ribbon streamers to something much more elaborate.

DECORATIONS FROM THE STORE-CUPBOARD

Before you rush to the shops to buy party decorations take a good look in the loft, the garage or at the back of your wardrobe for scraps and leftovers that can be given a new life as Halloween accessories.

WHITE SHEETS These can become tablecloths, either left white and decorated with black paper witches, cats and bats, or sprayed with gold and silver spray paint (perhaps left over from Christmas) through simple star and moon stencils cut from scraps of card (old cereal boxes would be ideal for this). Why not dye them black or dark blue with dye you can use in the washing machine?

PAINT You may have some gold, silver or white paint left over from Christmas, cans of car paint spray, or some coloured emulsion paint left from decorating. Use these materials to paint multicoloured witches and wizards, white skulls or ghosts on paper or fabric hangings.

WALLPAPER Paint Halloween figures on the back of old rolls of wallpaper and use any leftover packets of wallpaper adhesive for papier mâché heads and skulls.

FISHING LINE Transparent and strong, unwanted fishing line is ideal for hanging decorations from the ceiling.

TWIGS Collected from the garden (not picked from the wild), dried twigs can be left natural or sprayed with white, silver or black paint. Place bunches of twigs in pots and hang spooky plastic or edible decorations from them.

STREAMERS

Make folded paper-chain streamers of ghosts, cats, pumpkins and witches. Just choose the length and width you want and cut strips of coloured paper accordingly. Fold the paper strips, backwards and forwards, concertina fashion, then draw your chosen shape on the top piece. Cut out the shape, remembering to leave two small areas on each side of the design at the folded edges uncut, so that the streamer can be opened out to form one long chain. Drape at the window, around the door or pin to the front of the table.

A WITCHY WELCOME

Attach a card skeleton arm and hand through your letterbox to greet your guests and prop up a witch's broom by the door. Cut out black witch silhouettes from paper or card and hang them at your front windows with a low lamp on in the room.

CREEPY CROCKERY

Give old white china and glassware a new lease of life by painting on Halloween motifs with coloured glass paints. First outline your design with gold relief outline paint,

Disposable Halloween tableware is a boon for a large party, saving time and effort when it comes to clearing away.

available from good art shops, and pipe straight from the tube. When dry fill the outlined areas with coloured glass paints using a fine paintbrush. As these paints won't withstand too much heavy use, decorate the edges of plates only and avoid areas that will come into contact with food or drink.

PLACE MATS

 If you have young children it can be great fun for them to help you to decorate shapes of coloured card with foil stars, sequins, lengths of foil ribbon or tinsel or small cut-out paper shapes, stuck on with dots of PVA glue.

The size of the place mat should be a little larger than a standard dinner plate, although you can choose any shape you like – from a simple star or moon, to a bat or ghost, or a spider with folded and raised legs, or a witch or wizard's face with hair and furry eyebrows. If you are just having a small gathering, you may like to make a different design for each place setting.

PUMPKIN PUNCH BOWL

If you have a very large pumpkin, it can be fun to fill the centre with a clear glass or plastic bowl and fill with cold punch, mulled wine or soup. But make sure that the bowl is level and pack the base if needed with folded kitchen foil.

SPINE-CHILLING ICE CUBES

Give drinks a spooky look with these creepy ice cube ideas.

FROZEN HANDS Fill up a latex glove with plain or coloured water and freeze until solid. Cut the glove away (or leave on) and add to a glass serving bowl or jug of chilled punch or fruit juice.
ICE BUGS Add edible jelly 'bugs' to sections of an ice cube tray filled with plain or coloured water. Freeze until solid then turn out and add to drinks.

EYEBALLS Half-fill sections of an ice cube tray with water. Add a halved green grape and press a raisin into it to create a horrible 'eye ball'. Freeze.
FESTIVE COLOURED CUBES Fill different ice cube trays with fruit juices of different flavours and colours, such as orange, cranberry and apple juice. Or make up your own more gruesome colours by adding black, green or blue paste food colourings to orange or apple juice.

Thirst-quenching drinks are a must.

Muslin ghost

This fun ghost looks great suspended from the ceiling or inside a window. If you hang it using fishing line, it really will look as if it's flying through the air. For a party, make up five or six ghosts and hang at different heights for an even spookier effect.

YOU WILL NEED

50 x 146 cm (20 x 57 inches) fine white muslin
1 thin metal coat hanger
adhesive tape
1 balloon, blown up
halved orange
2 tablespoons powdered all-purpose wallpaper paste
coloured paper
1 m (39 inches) fishing line

Cut five long strips about 5 cm (2 inches) wide from the selvage edge of the muslin. Twist the hook off the coat hanger then squeeze the hanger together to shape the ghost's arms. Bind the coat hanger with three muslin strips to conceal the wire, taping the ends of the muslin to secure.

With the remaining muslin strips and tape tie the balloon to the coat hanger, the balloon knot and pointed end of the hanger facing down-wards. Insert the end of the hanger into the orange so the ghost stands upright.

Cut 2 squares from the remaining muslin, one 50 cm (20 inches) and one 32 cm (13 inches). Cut the rest of the muslin into small odd-shaped rectangles.

Mix 500 ml (17 fl oz) water with the wallpaper paste according to the packet instructions.

Dip the largest piece of muslin into the paste and squeeze so

that the paste penetrates thoroughly. Scoop off any excess then drape the muslin over the balloon. Continue to add muslin until the frame and balloon are completely covered. Make sure there are at least three layers over the balloon. Leave to dry for two days.

Cut the face and mouth out of the top layer of muslin using small sharp scissors, leaving the balloon intact. Cut similar shapes from the coloured paper and tape in place under the top layer of muslin.

Stitch the fishing line securely to the top of the head. Remove the orange and fold up and tape the pointed end of the coat hanger for safety. Suspend from a hook in the ceiling.

Preparation time: 40 minutes
Drying time: 2 days
Finishing time: 15 minutes

Pumpkin lanterns

Pumpkin lanterns epitomize Halloween and make a wonderful table centrepiece or can serve as a welcome in a window or on the front door step. Use one large pumpkin or choose several smaller ones and make a lantern for each child. Carved pumpkins also make festive plant containers (see opposite).

YOU WILL NEED
pumpkin
large cook's knife
large kitchen spoon
small sharp-pointed knife
night-light candle

Cut a thick slice off the top of the pumpkin using a large cook'sknife to make a hole large enough to get your hand in. Reserve the top slice for the lid.

Scoop out the seeds from the centre of the pumpkin using a large spoon and discard them, along with any long fibrous threads. Carefully cut and spoon out the pumpkin flesh, making sure that you leave a wall about 2.5 cm (1 inch) thick. Reserve the pumpkin flesh and use in the recipes on pages 24, 32, 33, 34 and 47.

Lightly mark facial features such as eyes, nose, mouth and jagged teeth using a small pointed knife. Cut around the lines and through the pumpkin wall. If the design is complicated, you may find it easier to cut away small sections at a time.

Carve eyebrows, hair or whiskers by cutting off the dark orange skin to reveal a paler layer of pumpkin below, without cutting right through the pumpkin wall.

Place a night-light candle inside the pumpkin. Light the candle when ready and replace the pumpkin lid.

Preparation time: **45 minutes**

Halloween lanterns

Transform a few old empty glass jars into these striking lanterns to hold night-light candles. These make an eye-catching decoration on the steps up to a front door or on the mantelpiece. This is a project that the kids can help with.

Autumn leaves

YOU WILL NEED

small and large orange beads
heavy-gauge fuse wire
clean glass jar
yellow cellophane
adhesive tape
glue gun
wire cutters
yellow skeleton leaves
dried bracken leaves
night-light candle

Thread the tiny orange beads on to wire. Twist the wire around the top of a glass jar and then up to make a handle, twisting the ends together to secure tightly and cutting off surplus wire with wire cutters.

Thread larger plastic beads on to more wire and then twist around the handle. Secure tightly.

Cut a strip of cellophane the same height and circumference as the jar and tape in place. Using a glue gun, run a line of glue down the spine of each skeleton leaf and stick on to the cellophane at angles so they overlap slightly. Do the same with the bracken leaves and stick over the first layer of leaves. Add a night-light to the lantern.

Preparation time: **45 minutes**

VARIATIONS
Paper patchwork

Replace the leaves with coloured fibre paper torn into small squares. Stick rows of alternate colours around the glass jar using a glue gun.

Jewelled lantern

Liven up a plain hanging lantern by adding small and large beads as in Autumn Leaves project, left.

Starry night

Customize small plain glass tumblers by piping on stars, dots and wavy lines with gold relief outline paint squeezed straight from the tube. When dry fill in with blue glass paint using a small paintbrush. Leave for 1 hour to dry then add a small night-light to each.

Trick or treat carriers

These eye-catching carriers for treats or tricks can be as wild or adventurous as you and your little helpers want to make them.

Materials are for one carrier: increase as necessary for the number of children in your party.

Ribbon lattice

YOU WILL NEED

2 litre (3½ pint) round plastic bottle, well washed

3 m (3¼ yards) x 1.5 cm (¾ inch) wide black satin ribbon

adhesive tape

2 m (2¼ yards) x 1.5 cm (¾ inch) wide orange satin ribbon

36 cm (14 inches) x 5 mm (¼ inch) wide orange cord

🕷 Trim off the top of the bottle to form a container about 12 cm (5 inches) deep. Make two holes opposite each other about 1.5 cm (¾ inch) from the top of the carrier.

🕷 Cut the black ribbon into 15 cm (6 inch) lengths. Stick one strip vertically to the side of the container so that the ribbon folds over the top and bottom edges of the container and secure with adhesive tape. Lay a second vertical ribbon next to the first, stick and repeat until the container is completely covered and no plastic is visible.

🕷 Starting at the top of the container, weave the orange ribbon (no need to cut yet) horizontally over and under the black ribbon strips. Pin the ends together and snip off the excess ribbon. Weave a second line of

orange ribbon, beginning one black ribbon strip to the left of the first one so that alternate lines of black ribbon are covered. Continue until the carrier is completely covered. Sew the pinned ends of orange ribbon together and slide under the black ribbon strips to conceal the seams.

🕷 Thread the cord through the pierced holes to make a handle. Knot the ends or secure with tape on the inside.

Preparation time: 45 minutes

Box of tricks

YOU WILL NEED

1 litre (1¾ pint) rectangular plastic
    container, well washed
double-sided tape
120 cm (48 inches) x 2.5 cm (1 inch)
    wide black satin ribbon
120 cm (48 inches) x 2.5 cm (1 inch)
    wide orange satin ribbon
orange foil pumpkin confetti
    (available from stationery stores)
16 black mirror motifs (available
    from haberdashery departments)
PVA glue or glue gun
36 cm (14 inches) x 5 mm (¼ inch)
    wide orange cord

Cut the plastic container to make a carrier 10 cm (4 inches) deep. Make two holes in opposite sides for a handle.

Cover the four corners of the container with double-sided tape. Stick alternate horizontal strips of black and orange ribbon around the sides. Trim to fit and secure the ribbon overlap with another strip of double-sided tape.

Stick foil confetti and mirror decorations on to the ribbon with a little PVA glue or a glue gun. Thread the cord through the pierced holes for the handle and knot the ends on the inside.

Preparation time: **30 minutes**

VARIATION
Fierce and feathery

You can vary the size of the container. The one used here is a 3.6 litre (6 pint) plastic carton. Cut below the handle on the carton to give a carrier 10 cm (4 inches) high. Decorate with black feathers, ribbons and pompons.

Horrible hands

A great talking point as place card or sweet holders, these hands can be as wacky as you wish to make them.

YOU WILL NEED

1 disposable (surgical) latex glove
300 ml (½ pint) cold water
500 g (1 lb) plaster of Paris
red or purple acrylic paint
fake pink plastic nails
black nail varnish
super glue or glue gun
black feathers and/or small pieces
   of black fake fur
coloured card

Use curved hands as fun sweet holders.

Blow into the glove then squeeze out the air. Stretch the top of the glove over a tall jug so that the fingers hang down inside. Secure with pegs. The glove will swell slightly when filled, so make sure the container is wide enough for you to be able to remove the glove later!

Put the water in a bowl and gradually sprinkle 425 g (14 oz) of the plaster into the water. Allow to stand for 1 minute then mix gently until smooth to avoid creating air bubbles.

Quickly pour the mixture into the glove, carefully releasing the glove from one side of the container if the mixture forms an air lock. Carefully lift the glove out and twist the top to stop the plaster falling out, secure with a peg. Dry flat, or shape the hand in a small bowl that will support the fingers in the position you want. Leave to set overnight. When the plaster is set hard, slit the glove down the centre and peel off. Smooth any rough edges with fine sandpaper (mend any broken fingers or fill any air holes with extra plaster).

Thin the paint if necessary with a few drops of water and paint the hand. Set aside until completely dry.

Mix a tablespoon of plaster with enough water to make a paste, use to stick on the nails. Leave to harden for 1 hour then paint the nails with nail varnish. Use dots of super glue to stick feathers or fur to the back of the hand and knuckles. Add a folded place card.

Preparation time: **45 minutes**
Drying time: **overnight**

spooky wind chimes

Give an old wind chime a face lift or buy a really cheap one and use the hook, pendulum and metal rods threaded together with this baked salt dough decoration. Hang your wind chime in the doorway, next to a window or above the table for some added spookiness.

YOU WILL NEED

250 g (8 oz) plain flour
275 g (9 oz) salt
1 tablespoon powdered all-purpose
  wallpaper paste
blue, purple, black, white, green and
  gold acrylic paints
plastic eye and glue
matt polyurethane varnish
small beads and fine gold beading
  thread or fishing line
1 wind chime, unthreaded
length of narrow ribbon

Mix the flour, salt and wallpaper paste together. Measure out 200 ml (7 fl oz) cold water. Pour in half the water, then gradually mix in the rest as needed to give a smooth firm dough.

Knead the dough well on a clean work surface for 5 minutes until smooth, adding more flour if sticky. Wrap the dough in a plastic bag and leave to rest for 30 minutes.

Knead the dough for 2–3 minutes, roll out on a floured surface until 1 cm (½ inch) thick. Cut out a 12 cm (5 inch) circle using a small saucer as a guide and cut out large stars with a biscuit cutter. Put the shapes on a baking sheet lined with non-stick baking paper. Cut two tiny stars and press on to the edge of the large circle.

To decorate the dough circle, mould a broomstick about 11 cm (4½ inches) long and wrap the end with a 6 x 12 cm (2½ x 5 inch) strip of dough cut into a fringe. Shape dough trimmings into the witch's head, body, arms and legs and attach these to the dough circle. Cut a cloak, dress, hat and shoes from thinly rolled out dough. To make the hair, press the dough through a sieve and lift on to the witch using a knife. Mark five holes along the bottom edge of the dough circle and two at the top, and one in each of the large star shapes using a skewer.

Bake the shapes at 110ºC (225ºF), Gas Mark ¼, for at least 9 hours until the dough has completely dried out. Remake the holes if needed and leave to cool completely.

Dilute some blue paint, then paint the circle. Leave to dry for at least 1 hour, then build up the other colours, first the purple dress, then the black cloak, shoes and hat. Mix black and white paint for the hair and use green for the face and arms and gold for the stars. When dry, stick a plastic eye in place and paint on a black mouth. Leave to dry completely. Paint on three coats of varnish, letting each dry before adding the next.

Thread beads on to beading thread or fishing line and hold in place with knots. Add to the circle with the rethreaded metal rods and the dough stars. Hang the circle by some ribbon.

Preparation time: **1 hour**
Cooking time: **9 hours or overnight**
Decoration time: **45 minutes**

VARIATION
Ghost chime

Adapt this idea to make a ghost-shaped design. Spiders could also be made by shaping balls of dough into small domes. Paint red then mark holes in the sides for lengths of black pipe cleaners to be glued in for the legs.

Pumpkin and sage soup with bat croûtons

Mild, creamy and velvety smooth, this delicious soup, speckled with just a hint of sage is ideal for parties with guests of all ages. This recipe is an ideal way of using up leftovers from the Pumpkin Lanterns (see page 14).

YOU WILL NEED

3 tablespoons sunflower oil
50 g (2 oz) butter
1 large onion, chopped
750 g (1½ lb) pumpkin flesh, chopped
2 tablespoons chopped sage
2 cloves garlic, chopped (optional)
900 ml (1½ pints) vegetable or chicken stock
300 ml (½ pint) milk
300 ml (½ pint) single cream
3 slices white bread
paprika
salt and freshly ground black pepper

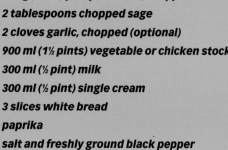 Heat 1 tablespoon of the oil and half of the butter in a large saucepan, add the onion and fry for 5 minutes until lightly browned. Add the pumpkin, sage and garlic, if using, and fry for 3 minutes, stirring. Pour in the stock, season and bring to the boil. Cover and simmer for 30 minutes.

Purée the soup in batches in a food processor or liquidizer. Return to the pan and stir in the milk and half the cream.

Cut the bread into six bat shapes using a small metal biscuit cutter, or cut around your own cardboard template.

When almost ready to serve, reheat the soup gently and heat the remaining oil and butter in a frying pan. Add the bread shapes and fry for 2 minutes on each side until golden then drain on kitchen paper. Ladle the soup into bowls, swirl the remaining cream over the top, sprinkle with paprika and add the croûtons.

Serves 6
Preparation time: **20 minutes**
Cooking time: **40 minutes**

Tomato and thyme focaccia sticks

This rustic-style bread is easy to make with no-soak, no-froth easy-blend yeast. It is delicious served warm with Pumpkin and Sage Soup (see opposite).

YOU WILL NEED

650 g (1 lb 5 oz) strong plain (bread) flour
2 teaspoons coarse sea salt
4 tablespoons olive oil
20 g (¾ oz) or small bunch thyme
7 g (¼ oz) sachet easy-blend dried yeast
up to 500 ml (17 fl oz) warm water
3 tablespoons sun-dried tomato paste
3 tablespoons grated Parmesan cheese

Put the flour and half of the salt in a bowl. Drizzle 3 tablespoons of the oil around the edge of the bowl and sprinkle half the thyme leaves and all the yeast into the middle. Gradually mix in enough warm water to make a soft, but not sticky dough.

Knead the dough on a lightly floured surface for 10 minutes until it is smooth and elastic. Put it back into the bowl and cover. Leave to rise in a warm place for 45 minutes or until doubled in size.

Knead the dough again for 5 minutes then cut it into three equal pieces. Roll each piece into a rough oval about 30 cm (12 inches) long.

Spread the dough with sun-dried tomato paste and sprinkle with Parmesan. Roll up along the long edges to form three long thin sticks. Place on a greased baking sheet. Prick with a skewer, drizzle with the remaining oil and sprinkle with the remaining salt and thyme leaves. Allow to rise for about 15 minutes.

Bake the loaves in a preheated oven, 220°C (425°F), Gas Mark 7, for 15–20 minutes or until golden brown and the bases sound hollow when tapped. Serve straight from the oven or reheat when needed.

Makes 3 loaves
Preparation time: **30 minutes**
Rising time: **1 hour**
Cooking time: **15–20 minutes**

Honey-glazed pork

For a more formal dinner, try this delicious pork with crispy crackling with a sticky honey, fennel and chilli glaze.

YOU WILL NEED

2 kg (4 lb) lean rolled leg or shoulder of pork
4 tablespoons olive oil
2 teaspoons coarse sea salt
1 teaspoon roughly crushed black peppercorns
1 tablespoon fennel seeds, roughly crushed
1.5 kg (3 lb) baking potatoes, cut into chunks
500 g (1 lb) parsnips, cut into chunks
500 g (1 lb) carrots, cut into chunks
3 onions, halved, leaving root intact
4 cloves garlic, roughly chopped
2–3 dried red chillies (optional)
3 red dessert apples
3 tablespoons clear honey
3 tablespoons plain flour
250 ml (8 fl oz) white wine
500 ml (17 fl oz) chicken stock
sage leaves, to garnish

Score the pork skin (if not already done) with a very sharp knife. Put into a roasting tin and rub with a little olive oil, salt, pepper and half the fennel seeds. Bake in a preheated oven, 220°C (425°F), Gas Mark 7, for 20 minutes. Reduce the heat to 200°C (400°F), Gas Mark 6, and cook for 2 hours or 30 minutes per 500 g (1 lb).

Meanwhile, parboil the potatoes in boiling water for 5 minutes and drain. Add the potatoes, parsnips, carrots, onions, garlic, chillies, if using, and the remaining oil to the roasting tin when the meat has been in the oven for 45 minutes. Coat the vegetables in the meat juices, sprinkle with the remaining fennel seeds and roast them, turning once.

After 2 hours at the lower temperature, add the apples to the tin. Turn the vegetables and spoon over the juices. Drizzle the pork, vegetables and apples with the honey. Roast for a further 10 minutes or until the pork juices run clear when the thickest part of the joint is pierced with a skewer.

Place the pork, vegetables and apples on a serving plate. Put the roasting tin on the hob and stir the flour into the juices. Cook for 1 minute then gradually mix in the wine and stock, scraping up the residues from the bottom of the tin. Bring to the boil, stirring, until the sauce is thickened and smooth. Pour into a jug and serve with the sliced pork and vegetables, garnished with sage leaves.

Serves 6
Preparation time: **25 minutes**
Cooking time: 2½ **hours**

Pumpkin fondue

This rich cheesy fondue is a warming alternative to cold dips for an informal Halloween party and is a great talking point as the fondue is served in small baked pumpkins. Serve with dipping skewers and spoons so that the pumpkin flesh can be scooped out once the fondue has been eaten.

YOU WILL NEED

2 small pumpkins
2 tablespoons olive oil
½ bunch spring onions, trimmed, finely sliced
1 clove garlic, crushed
250 g (8 oz) Emmenthal cheese, grated
250 g (8 oz) Gruyère cheese, grated
200 ml (7 fl oz) dry white wine or cider
1 tablespoon cornflour, mixed to a smooth
  paste with a little water
grated nutmeg
paprika
a few dried chilli flakes (optional)
salt and freshly ground black pepper

TO SERVE

apple slices
celery chunks
cubes of bread

Cut a slice off the top of each pumpkin and scoop out the seeds. Scoop out some of the flesh to give pumpkin shells with walls about 1 cm (½ inch) thick.

Brush the inside of each pumpkin with 2 teaspoons of the oil then put on a baking sheet and bake with the lid back in position in a preheated oven, 180°C (350°F), Gas Mark 4, for 30 minutes.

Heat the remaining oil in a saucepan, add most of the spring onions and all of the garlic and cook for 2–3 minutes until softened. Add the cheeses, wine or cider and cornflour paste to the saucepan. Season with salt, pepper and a little grated nutmeg. Heat gently, stirring constantly until the cheese has melted into a smooth sauce. Take off the heat and set aside.

Before serving, reheat the fondue, pour into the baked pumpkins and sprinkle with the remaining spring onions and a little paprika and chilli flakes, if using. Serve with apple, celery and cubed bread for dunking.

Serves 4–6
Preparation time: **30 minutes**
Cooking time: **30 minutes**

Radicchio salad with blue cheese dressing

Radicchio leaves add an exotic flash of red to this crisp crunchy salad. If you'd like to make this in advance, then prepare the beetroot mixture, dressing and eggs earlier in the day and just assemble a few minutes before you plan to eat. To create an extra ghoulish effect, cut the eggs in half and arrange cut side down on the salad, coat with dressing and add a halved black olive for an eyeball.

YOU WILL NEED

1 head of radicchio, separated into leaves
250 g (8 oz) cooked beetroot, finely diced
2 carrots, coarsely grated
½ red onion, finely chopped
2 celery sticks, finely diced
6 hard-boiled eggs, shelled
small sprigs of parsley, to garnish

DRESSING

150 g (5 oz) creamy blue cheese,
 rind removed
6 tablespoons single cream
150 g (5 oz) natural yogurt
salt and freshly ground black pepper

Divide the radicchio between six serving plates. Mix the beetroot, carrot, red onion and celery together in a bowl.

To make the dressing mash two-thirds of the blue cheese with a fork then work in the cream and yogurt or process in a blender or food processor until smooth, adding a little seasoning at the end. Toss with the beetroot salad and spoon on to the radicchio leaves.

Cut the eggs into wedges and arrange over the salad. Crumble the remaining cheese over each plate, add a little black pepper and garnish with sprigs of parsley.

Serves 6
Preparation time: **15 minutes**

Bean pot supper

This easy one-pot dish is great for informal suppers. It can be cooked in advance and kept warm until you are ready to eat.

YOU WILL NEED

2 tablespoons sunflower oil
625 g (1¼ lb) lean leg or fillet of lamb, diced
2 onions, roughly chopped
2 cloves garlic, crushed
2 teaspoons hot (picante) Spanish paprika
1 teaspoon caraway seeds
½ teaspoon ground cinnamon
2 tablespoons plain flour
2 tablespoons light muscovado sugar
400 g (13 oz) can tomatoes
425 g (14 oz) can red kidney beans, drained
425 g (14 oz) can mixed pulses, borlotti or
   cannellini beans, drained
600 ml (1 pint) chicken stock
500 g (1 lb) pumpkin flesh, diced
250 ml (8 fl oz) soured cream or
   Greek-style yogurt
paprika
salt and freshly ground black pepper

SALSA

1 red dessert apple, diced
1 tablespoon lemon juice
½ red pepper, deseeded and diced
½ red onion, finely chopped
large pinch caraway seeds

Heat the oil in a flameproof casserole and fry the lamb and chopped onions for 5 minutes, stirring until browned. Stir in the garlic and spices, cook for 1 minute then stir in the flour and sugar. Add the canned tomatoes, pulses, stock and salt and pepper and bring to the boil.

Cover the casserole and transfer to a preheated oven, 160°C (325°F), Gas Mark 3, for 1¼ hours. Add the pumpkin pieces, cover and cook for a further 1–1½ hours.

To make the salsa, toss the apple in the lemon juice and mix with the red pepper, onion and caraway seeds.

Serve on warmed plates, accompanied by spoonfuls of salsa and soured cream or yogurt sprinkled with paprika. Serve with baked potatoes or rice.

Serves 6
Preparation time: **25 minutes**
Cooking time: **2½–3 hours**

Cinnamon and pumpkin muffins

These muffins can be eaten hot or cold. It can be fun to get your guests to guess the magic ingredient – the pumpkin has such a mild taste that they may think that these muffins are made with apricots!

YOU WILL NEED

200 g (7 oz) diced pumpkin
300 g (10 oz) plain flour
3 teaspoons baking powder
1½ teaspoons ground cinnamon
150 g (5 oz) caster sugar
4 tablespoons sunflower oil
2 tablespoons milk
3 eggs
150 g (5 oz) natural yogurt
50 g (2 oz) raisins
50 g (2 oz) sugar lumps, crushed

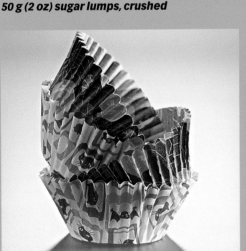

Line 12 sections of a deep muffin tin with paper cases. Steam the pumpkin pieces above a saucepan of boiling water for 5 minutes until just tender.

Put all the dry ingredients (except the sugar lumps) in a large mixing bowl. Mix the oil, milk and eggs together then add to the dry ingredients along with the yogurt. Roughly fork the ingredients together.

Add the steamed pumpkin and raisins. Stir until just mixed then spoon into the paper cases. Sprinkle with the crushed sugar lumps and bake in a preheated oven, 200°C (400°F), Gas Mark 6, for 18–20 minutes until well risen and golden.

Makes 12
Preparation time: **20 minutes**
Cooking time: **23–25 minutes**

Maple pumpkin pie

What better or more traditional way to use up the pumpkin from a hollowed-out lantern than in this custard-based tart?

YOU WILL NEED

250 g (8 oz) plain flour
75 g (3 oz) butter
50 g (2 oz) vegetable shortening
cold water, to mix
4 eggs, beaten
500 g (1 lb) pumpkin, diced
175 g (6 oz) light muscovado sugar
125 ml (4 fl oz) maple syrup
1 teaspoon ground ginger
1 teaspoon ground cinnamon, plus extra for
*   sprinkling*
large pinch grated nutmeg
250 ml (8 fl oz) double cream

Place the flour in a bowl, add the butter and shortening and rub in using your fingertips until the mixture resembles fine breadcrumbs. Add enough cold water (about 3 tablespoons) to mix to a soft dough. Turn out on to a lightly floured surface and knead briefly. Roll out a little larger than a 23 cm (9 inch) flan case. Line the greased flan case with the pastry. Press the pastry into the base and sides of the case and trim off any excess. Chill for 15 minutes.

Shape some of the pastry trimmings into a 'rope' 1 x 30 cm (½ x 12 inches) long then cut into six pieces for broomstick handles. Roll the remainder into a 7 x 18 cm (3 x 7 inch) rectangle. Cut the rectangle in half lengthways, then cut each strip into three lengths. Fringe the edges with a small knife then wrap around the broomstick handles.

Line the pastry case with a large piece of greaseproof paper, fill with baking beans and bake in a preheated oven, 190°C (375°F), Gas Mark 5, for 15 minutes. Place the broomsticks on a baking sheet, brush with a little beaten egg and cook for 10 minutes.

Meanwhile, steam the pumpkin over a saucepan of boiling water for 10 minutes or until tender. Purée in a blender or food processor.

Mix the eggs, sugar, syrup, spices, half the cream and the pumpkin purée in a bowl. Lift the paper and beans out of the pastry case. Pour in the pumpkin mixture and bake for 35–40 minutes until set and golden.

Allow to cool. When cold whip the remaining cream and spread over the top of the pie, sprinkle with a little ground cinnamon and decorate with the pastry broomsticks.

Serves 6
Preparation time: **40 minutes**
Chilling time: **15 minutes**
Cooking time: **50–55 minutes**

Blueberry and port jelly

The inclusion of port gives this fruity jelly a sophisticated adult flavour. You could replace it with fruit juice for a non-alcoholic version suitable for children.

YOU WILL NEED

2 x 135 g (4½ oz) packets strawberry jelly
150 ml (¼ pint) boiling water
1 orange, squeezed
150 ml (¼ pint) ruby port
125 g (4 oz) blueberries
125 g (4 oz) seedless grapes, halved
single cream, to serve

Make up the jelly with the boiling water, then stir in the juice of the orange and the port. Make up to 600 ml (1 pint) with cold water. Leave to cool for 15 minutes then mix in the blueberries and grapes.

Spoon the mixture into six small individual moulds and chill until set.
Dip the moulds in hot water, count to 20 then release the edges of the jelly with your fingertips and invert each mould on to a plate. Serve with single cream.

Serves 6
Preparation time: **15 minutes**
Chilling time: **4 hours**

Watermelon and tequila granita

This wonderfully refreshing dessert can be made in advance. As the tequila is added only when the granita is served and can be omitted, this dessert is suitable for a mixed-age gathering and/or for adults who prefer to avoid alcohol.

YOU WILL NEED

1 small watermelon, about 3–3.5 kg (6–7 lb)
125 ml (4 fl oz) water
175 g (6 oz) granulated sugar
finely grated rind and juice of 2 limes
6 tablespoons tequila (optional)
lime rind, to decorate (optional)

 Cut the watermelon into quarters and scoop out the flesh. Purée briefly in batches in a blender or a food processor fitted with a plastic blade. Strain through a sieve and discard the seeds.

 Put the water and sugar in a saucepan and heat gently until the sugar has completely dissolved. Bring to the boil and cook for 1 minute. Cool then stir in the watermelon purée and the lime rind and juice.

 Pour into a pre-cooled electric ice-cream maker and churn for 40 minutes until stiff enough to spoon. Depending on the size of the machine, you may need to make the granita in two batches. Spoon into a plastic container and freeze until ready to serve. If you don't have an ice-cream maker, pour the mixture into a large freezer-proof dish to a depth of 2.5 cm (1 inch) and freeze for 4–6 hours until mushy around the edges. Beat with a fork to break up the ice crystals then return to the freezer for 2 hours, beating every 30 minutes until the mixture resembles crushed ice.

 Leave the granita at room temperature for 10 minutes before serving to soften slightly. Rough up with a fork and spoon into glasses. Decorate with curls of lime rind. Serve drizzled with tequila, if liked.

Serves 6
Preparation time: **20 minutes**
Cooking time: **5 minutes**
Freezing time: **40 minutes in an ice-cream maker/6–8 hours in a freezer**

Black magic cup

This spiced red-wine toddy will quickly warm you on your return from a chilly evening of trick or treating with your children.

YOU WILL NEED
750 ml bottle red wine
250 ml (8 fl oz) orange juice
500 ml (17 fl oz) water
4 tablespoons brandy
75 g (3 oz) granulated or caster sugar
1 orange
8 cloves
1 cinnamon stick, halved

Pour the wine, orange juice, water, brandy and sugar into a large saucepan. Cut the orange into eight wedges and spike each wedge with a clove and add to the pan with the halved cinnamon stick. Gently heat the wine for 10 minutes, being careful not to bring it to the boil.

Remove from the heat and leave to stand for at least 30 minutes (or several hours, if possible) to allow the flavours to mingle. Reheat for 3–4 minutes when needed, making sure not to boil it. Discard the cinnamon and ladle into heatproof glasses, adding an orange wedge to each.

Serves 8
Preparation time: **10 minutes**
Cooking time: **13–14 minutes**
Standing time: **30 minutes**

Ghoul's blood

This vibrant, blue adults-only cocktail will soon get your guests in the party mood. Serve with plenty of ice and an eyeball-like slice of kiwi fruit, if liked.

YOU WILL NEED
8 tablespoons white rum
8 tablespoons blue curaçao
150 ml (¼ pint) pineapple juice
ice cubes, to serve
1 kiwi fruit, peeled and sliced (optional), to decorate

Mix the rum, curaçao and pineapple juice together in a jug or cocktail shaker. Pour into glasses half-filled with ice and add a slice of kiwi fruit to each, if liked.

Serves 4
Preparation time: **5 minutes**

Spider web pizzas

Every kid loves pizza and what could be more fun than to turn pizzas into wicked-looking spider webs? If you'd rather not pipe on the ketchup web, squirt it straight from the plastic bottle.

YOU WILL NEED

625 g (1¼ lb) strong plain white flour
1 teaspoon salt
1 teaspoon caster sugar
7 g (¼ oz) sachet easy-blend dried yeast
350–400 ml (12–14 fl oz) warm water
3 tablespoons olive oil
6 tablespoons tomato ketchup
1 teaspoon dried marjoram or oregano
3 tomatoes, finely chopped
125 g (4 oz) frozen sweetcorn
250 g (8 oz) mozzarella cheese, grated

TO DECORATE
4 tablespoons tomato ketchup
black paste food colouring
12 cherry tomatoes
1 carrot or red pepper, cut into fine strips

Put the flour, salt, sugar and yeast in a bowl and gradually mix in the warm water and 1 tablespoon of the oil to form a soft dough. Turn out on to a floured surface and knead well for 10 minutes until elastic.

Divide the dough into 12 equal portions and roll out each into a round about 14 cm (5½ inches) in diameter. Place on oiled baking sheets and spread thinly with ketchup mixed with the herbs and the remaining oil. Sprinkle with the chopped tomato and sweetcorn and cover with cheese. Leave in a warm place to rise for 20–30 minutes.

Bake in a preheated oven, 200°C (400°F), Gas Mark 6, for 10 minutes until well risen and the cheese is bubbling. If you have trays on more than one shelf, swap these over halfway through cooking so that the pizzas cook evenly.

To decorate, colour the ketchup black with a little colouring and spoon into a greaseproof paper piping bag. When the pizzas are cooked, snip off the tip of the bag and pipe lines and concentric circles of black tomato ketchup to make a web design. Cut a thin slice off the stalk end of each tomato and place cut side down in the centre of each web. Arrange pepper or carrot strips around it for legs and add ketchup eyes.

Makes 12
Preparation time: **45 minutes**
Rising time: **20–30 minutes**
Cooking time: **10 minutes**
Decorating time: **10 minutes**

Witches' fingers

These chunky oven-roasted chips can be served as part of a buffet table, as a starter, or as a main course accompaniment, and are popular with children and adults alike.

YOU WILL NEED

1.5 kg (3 lb) baking potatoes, scrubbed
6 tablespoons olive oil
2 tablespoons plain flour
2 teaspoons coarse sea salt
1 teaspoon roughly crushed black
  peppercorns
paprika
6 stems rosemary, leaves torn from stems
4 cloves garlic, finely chopped

DIPPING SAUCE

6 tablespoons tomato ketchup
1 tablespoon Worcestershire sauce
1 teaspoon Dijon or mild mustard
a little hot chilli sauce
2 tablespoons water

Cut the potatoes into long wedge or finger shapes and parboil in a saucepan of boiling water for 4 minutes then drain.

Meanwhile heat the oil in a roasting tin in a preheated oven, 200°C (400°F), Gas Mark 6, for 5 minutes. Mix the flour, salt, pepper, paprika, rosemary leaves and garlic together in a large plastic bag, add the drained potato wedges and shake well.

Tip the coated potato wedges into the roasting tin and spoon over the hot oil. Return the tin to the oven for 45–55 minutes, turning once or twice until the potatoes are evenly browned.

Mix the dipping sauce ingredients together with 2 tablespoons of water in a small bowl and set on a large plate. Dip the ends of the potato wedges into the sauce to resemble red fingernails and arrange on the plate.

Serves 6
Preparation time: **15 minutes**
Cooking time: **50–60 minutes**

40

Nibbles

Children will love these quick-and-easy nibbles. Serve the Toasted Seeds with drinks or sprinkled over mashed potatoes or parsnips. The Gourmet Crisps are delicious served on their own for kids or with a soured cream and chive dip for adults.

Toasted seeds

YOU WILL NEED
2 teaspoons sunflower oil
50 g (2 oz) pumpkin seeds
50 g (2 oz) sunflower seeds
25 g (1 oz) flaked almonds
1 tablespoon runny honey
1 tablespoon soy sauce

 Heat the oil in a non-stick frying pan, add the seeds and almonds and cook, stirring, for 2 minutes until lightly browned.

 Take the pan off the heat, add the honey and soy sauce and stir. Return to the heat for 1 minute then leave to cool in the pan.

Serves 4
Preparation time: **2 minutes**
Cooking time: **3 minutes**

Gourmet crisps

YOU WILL NEED
625 g (1¼ lb) pumpkin or butternut squash
4 small raw beetroot
1 sweet potato
sunflower or vegetable oil, for deep-frying
sea salt (optional)

Peel the vegetables and, using a swivel-headed vegetable peeler, pare them into wafer-thin slices. Pat dry with kitchen paper. Half-fill a large heavy-based saucepan with oil and heat to 180°C (350°F). If the oil sizzles as soon as you drop in a vegetable slice, it is hot enough.

Gradually add half the vegetable slices to the oil and cook for 1–2 minutes until crisp and golden. Drain on kitchen paper. Cook the remainder in the same way. Toss the adult portions in a little sea salt and serve in a bowl lined with a paper napkin.

Serves 4–6
Preparation time: **15 minutes**
Cooking time: **6 minutes**

spooky cookies

Hang these hauntingly good ghostly cookies with ribbon from some twigs arranged in a tall vase.

YOU WILL NEED
75 g (3 oz) butter
3 tablespoons golden syrup
150 g (5 oz) light muscovado sugar
375 g (12 oz) plain flour
2 teaspoons bicarbonate of soda
1 teaspoon ground ginger
1 teaspoon ground cinnamon
1 egg, beaten
1–3 tablespoons milk

TO DECORATE
7 g (¼ oz) sachet dried egg white
4 tablespoons warm water
275 g (9 oz) icing sugar, sifted
black paste food colouring
1–2 teaspoons lemon or orange juice
red and black writing icing in tubes
fine ribbon

Melt the butter, syrup and sugar in a saucepan, stirring until smooth. Mix the flour, bicarbonate of soda and spices together and stir into the pan, adding the beaten egg and enough milk to make a smooth dough.

When cool enough to handle, knead the dough and roll it out on a lightly floured surface to a thickness of 5 mm (¼ inch). Cut out ghost and bat shapes using biscuit cutters or by cutting around your own card templates with a small knife. Transfer to a greased baking sheet.

Make holes in the top of each cookie with the end of a skewer, then bake for 8–10 minutes in a preheated oven, 180°C (350°F), Gas Mark 4, until the dough begins to darken. Remake the holes in the cookies while still soft. Leave to cool.

To decorate, mix the dried egg white to a smooth thin paste with a little warm water, according to the packet instructions. Gradually whisk in the sifted icing sugar.

Colour half the icing black. Spoon 2 tablespoons into a greaseproof paper piping bag and pipe an outline around the edge and around the holes of all the bat-shaped biscuits. Add a few drops of fruit juice to the remaining black icing and spread inside the piped lines. Do the same with white icing over the ghost-shaped biscuits.

When the icing has hardened, pipe on facial features using black writing icing for the ghosts and red for the bats. Thread fine ribbon through the holes and hang up to serve.

Makes 20
Preparation time: 30 minutes
Cooking time: 16–20 minutes
Decorating time: 15 minutes

Lantern cakes

These edible pumpkin-style Lantern Cakes, made from ready-made muffins, provide a colourful treat for a children's Halloween party.

YOU WILL NEED

7 g (¼ oz) sachet dried egg white
4 tablespoons warm water
2 tablespoons liquid glucose
500 g (1 lb) icing sugar, sifted
yellow and red paste food colouring
4 American-style muffins
4 tablespoons apricot jam, sieved
cornflour, for dusting

 Put the dried egg white in a large bowl and gradually mix to a thin smooth paste with the water. Add the liquid glucose and then gradually beat in the icing sugar with a wooden spoon, using your hands when the mixture becomes too stiff to stir, to make a smooth, soft, rollable icing.

Colour 50 g (2 oz) of the icing yellow and wrap it in cling film until required. Colour the remainder orange using yellow and red food colourings.

Remove the paper cases from the muffins. Spread the tops and sides of the muffins with the sieved jam, reserving a little.

Cut the orange icing into four pieces and roll out one piece on a surface dusted with cornflour to make a circle large enough to encase a muffin. Wrap the icing around the muffin to cover it completely. Trim off any excess. Cover the other three muffins in the same way.

Roll out the yellow icing and cut out jagged mouth shapes and triangles for eyes. Stick on to the side of the icing-covered cakes with a little jam. Roll trimmings of both colours into a short fat 'rope' and score with a knife. Cut the 'rope' into short lengths and stick them on top of each cake for pumpkin stalks. Leave to dry for 2–3 hours or overnight.

Makes 4
Preparation time: **40 minutes**
Drying time: **2–3 hours or overnight**

Wicked witches

These are guaranteed to bring a smile to any child's face. If you have more than four guests, make up a second batch with blue butter-icing faces and green apple bootlace or black liquorice bootlace hair instead.

YOU WILL NEED

75 g (3 oz) dark cooking chocolate, broken into pieces
4 ice-cream cones
4 chocolate-covered or plain digestive biscuits
50 g (2 oz) butter, softened
125 g (4 oz) icing sugar
1 teaspoon vanilla essence
green paste food colouring
4 American-style muffins
50 g (2 oz) strawberry bootlace sweets
4 assorted coloured dolly mixture sweets
4 jelly sweets
black writing icing

Melt the chocolate in a bowl over a saucepan of just boiled water. Trim the rounded tops off the ice-cream cones with a serrated knife and discard. Spread the melted chocolate over the biscuits and cones. Place the cones upside down on the biscuits to make the hats.

Beat the butter in a bowl to soften. Gradually mix in the icing sugar. Stir in the vanilla essence and a little green colouring. Take the paper cases off the muffins and spread the muffin tops and sides with the icing, reserving about 1 tablespoon. Cut the bootlaces into 12–15 cm (5–6 inch) lengths and press on to the muffins for hair. Use the dolly mixture sweets for eyes and jelly sweets for noses. Draw jagged mouths and other facial features with writing icing.

Now stick the hardened chocolate-coated hats on the witches' heads using the reserved butter icing.

Makes 4
Preparation time: 25 minutes

Meringue-topped pumpkin pies

These tiny pumpkin pies are easy for small children to pick up in their hands when cool. They can also be served warm in a bowl with a spoonful of vanilla ice-cream.

YOU WILL NEED

1 quantity prepared pastry (see Maple Pumpkin Pie, page 34)
200 g (7 oz) diced pumpkin
½ teaspoon ground ginger
½ teaspoon ground cinnamon
125 g (4 oz) caster sugar
2 eggs
125 ml (4 fl oz) double cream
2 egg whites

Roll out the prepared pastry and cut 18 x 7 cm (3 inch) fluted circles using a biscuit cutter. Use the pastry circles to line 18 greased muffin tins.

Steam the diced pumpkin over a saucepan of boiling water for 10 minutes or until tender. Purée the pumpkin in a blender or food processor and mix with the spices, half the sugar, the whole eggs and the cream. Pour the filling into the pastry cases and cook in a preheated oven, 190°C (375°F), Gas Mark 4, for 15–20 minutes until set and golden.

Remove the pies from the oven and reduce the oven temperature to 150°C (300°F), Gas Mark 2. Whisk the egg whites until they form stiff peaks. Gradually whisk in the remaining sugar, a dessertspoon at a time. Continue to whisk until the mixture is smooth and glossy. Spoon over the pies and return to the oven for 7–8 minutes until the meringue is set and lightly browned. Serve warm or cold.

Makes 18
Preparation time: 40 minutes
Cooking time: 32–38 minutes

Black cat jelly

This grisly-looking fruit jelly is set inside a hollowed-out watermelon, carved to resemble the head of a witch's cat.

YOU WILL NEED

1 small watermelon, about 3–3.5 kg (6–7 lb)
2 x 135 g (4½ oz) packets strawberry jelly
300 ml (½ pint) boiling water
200 g (7 oz) frozen mixed raspberries, blackberries and strawberries
50 g (2 oz) strawberry bootlace sweets
50 g (2 oz) red jelly sweets
3 white pipe cleaners
1 glacé cherry

Mark two cat's ears near the top of the watermelon. Cut between and around the ears and remove the top of the melon in the same way as you would to make a pumpkin lantern. Scoop out the insides and use the flesh for another recipe (see Watermelon and Tequila Granita, page 36) or just eat it!

Mark cat features on the skin of the melon, then cut the top layer of skin away to reveal pale green flesh below. Be careful not to cut right through the melon wall or the jelly will run out!

Cut the jelly into cubes and dissolve in the boiling water, or as specified on the packet. Top up with cold water to make 900 ml (1½ pints). Leave to cool.

Put half the frozen fruit in the base of the melon, top with unravelled bootlace sweets. Add the remaining fruit and jelly sweets. Pour on the cooled jelly and transfer to the fridge for 4 hours or until set.

When ready to serve add curled pipe cleaner whiskers and a cherry nose to the front of the melon, securing with a cocktail stick, but remove it just before serving.

Serves 6
Preparation time: **30 minutes**
Chilling time: **4 hours**

These non-alcoholic drinks are great for partygoers of all ages, and really refreshing for thirsty children. The gruesome-looking Bleeding Heart is packed with vitamins. It's a great way of fooling the kids into drinking something that is really good for them!

Creepy cranberry crush

YOU WILL NEED

1 litre (1¾ pints) cranberry juice
500 ml (17 fl oz) apple juice
1 litre (1¾ pints) fizzy lemonade
1 red apple, cored, sliced and dipped
*   in lemon juice*
ice, to serve

 Mix all the liquid ingredients in a bowl. Pour into tall glasses half-filled with ice.

 Cut the apple slices into jagged teeth shapes and add one to each drink or balance over the edge of each glass.

Serves 6
Preparation time: **10 minutes**

Bleeding heart

YOU WILL NEED

100 g (3½ oz) raspberries, defrosted if frozen
2 bananas
4 tablespoons fromage frais
500 ml (17 fl oz) chilled orange juice

 Whizz the raspberries in a blender or food processor. Sieve if liked and then divide between four glasses.

Rinse the blender or food processor then whizz together the bananas, fromage frais and half the orange juice. Mix in the remaining orange juice and gently pour into the prepared glasses. Lightly swirl the raspberry and banana mixtures together with a knife then serve.

Serves 4
Preparation time: **10 minutes**

Face painting

Young children love to have their faces made up. It can be even more fun if they decorate each other or an older brother or sister helps out. If you have a child with very sensitive skin, test a small area of skin with the face paints 24 hours before using fully.

YOU WILL NEED
face paints in different colours, depending on selected design
make-up sponges
paintbrush

Pumpkin

Cover the face with an orange base, applied with a moistened make-up sponge. Leave to dry for a minute or two, then paint on black triangular eyes and a jagged mouth.

Spider's web

Cover the face with a white base, applied with a moistened make-up sponge. Leave to dry for a minute or two, then paint on black lines for a spider's web. Stitch coloured pipe cleaners to a black pompon to make a spider, adding moving toy eyes and secure it to the child's cheek with strips of surgical tape.

Skull

Cover the face with a white base, applied with a moistened make-up sponge. Leave for a minute or two, then wash the sponge and use it to apply black or grey shading around the mouth and under the cheekbones. Paint black circles around the eyes and alternating white and black squares around the mouth to look like white teeth with shadows between. Paint on black cracks or drizzles of blood red paint, if liked.

Vampire bat

Cover the face with a base of orange or red paint, applied with a moistened make-up sponge. Leave for a minute or two, then paint on a bat-wing shape over the eyes and nose with black paint. Make a black, black and silver, or red pompon into a bat head by sticking on moving toy eyes (available from haberdashery stores) and triangles of felt or paper for ears. Stick to the nose with a small strip of surgical tape.

Witch

Cover the face with a base colour of green, applied using a moistened make-up sponge. Allow to dry for a minute or two, then add blue over the cheekbones, chin and centre of forehead. Outline the eyes with blue, using a fine brush, then add zig-zag lines for scary eyebrows. Add extra paint under the eyes and fill in the eyelids with more blue, if liked. Add black dots below the eyes and paint the lips black.

Devil

Cover the face with a red base, applied with a moistened make-up sponge. Leave to dry for a minute or two, then paint on exaggerated black bushy eyebrows and outline eyes, lips and fangs. Paint inside fangs white then add some tear-drop shapes of red paint. Fill in the lips with purple or black paint.

Dracula

Cover the face with a green base, applied with a moistened make-up sponge. Wash the sponge then dip it in red paint and use to shade around the eyes. Paint on drops of blood around the mouth with red paint. Paint on angled black eyebrows. Complete the look with plastic vampire teeth.

Cat

Cover the face with a black base, making it lighter towards the centre by dipping the sponge in a little white paint. Leave to dry for a minute or two, then paint on vertical white eyebrows, a white nose area around the child's mouth and nose and white whiskers. Paint in some orange whiskers and dots around the mouth.

Dressing up

It can be fun and rewarding to make Halloween fancy dress outfits at home. Such costumes needn't be tricky or too time-consuming to undertake and will make your child look just that little bit more individual at the party.

Skeleton

Transform a few old black garments from your child's wardrobe into this bone-chilling costume.

YOU WILL NEED
black polo-necked, long-sleeved
   cotton T-shirt
black trousers
1 m (39 inches) x 90 cm (36 inches)
   white iron-on Vylene
black knitted hat
black socks and gloves
plastic skull mask or face paints
   (see page 50)

Mark the position of your child's elbows and knees on the T-shirt and trousers with pins. Measure the length of your child's main bones in the arms and legs. With a pencil draw bone shapes of the appropriate length on to the white iron-on Vylene.

Cut out the bones and iron them in position on to the clothes with the shiny side of the Vylene facing downwards. Complete the outfit with black socks and gloves and a black hat pulled right down over the hair and a plastic skull mask or skull face-paint design (see page 50).

Ghost

This simple design is made with an old white sheet and is ideal for children who are reluctant to dress up, as they can wear everyday clothes underneath and just take off the disguise when they like.

YOU WILL NEED
1 old white single bed sheet
pins, needle and white thread
30 cm (12 inch) square of black felt or
   other non-fraying fabric
white socks
white gym shoes

Fold the sheet in half then drape it over the child's head. Pin diagonal lines under each arm, working from each armpit down to the wrist, so that the sleeves are large and tapered and hang slightly over the child's hands. Mark where the sheet should be trimmed level with the floor.

Take the sheet off the child and, starting at the hem line, cut the sheet in a curve up to the wrist. Repeat on the other side. Turn over the raw edges and machine stitch, if liked. Hand or machine stitch the pinned lines for the sleeves.

Cut a jagged mouth and large oval eye shapes from the black felt. Machine or hand stitch on to the sheet in the position of your child's features. Cut out the centre of each shape so your child can see and speak. Complete with white socks and shoes.

Witch

Team an ordinary black T-shirt and tights into something very spooky with this easy-to-make black cloak and net skirt.

YOU WILL NEED

CLOAK

1.5 m (1¾ yards) x 115 cm (45 inches) **black sequinned velvet or heavy black lining fabric**

1.5 m (1¾ yards) x 115 cm (45 inches) **purple or blue lightweight shimmering fabric**

1.5 m (1¾ yards) x 2.5 cm (1 inch) **black bias binding**

1.5 m (1¾ yards) x 2.5 cm (1 inch) **wide black satin ribbon**

plastic bats and spiders on elastic (optional)

SKIRT

2 m (2¼ yards) x 137 cm (54 inches) **wide black net**

1 m (39 inches) x 2.5 cm (1 inch) wide **black cotton tape**

To make the cloak, pin the black and coloured fabric, right sides together, along two long edges and one short edge then machine stitch. Turn out the right way to make a 'bag' and press the seams flat.

Make a casing by pinning the bias binding across the cloak 15 cm (6 inches) down from the short stitched edge, then machine stitch in place along both long edges, leaving ends open. Pin a safety pin to one end of the satin ribbon, fold lengthways and thread through the bias binding. Pull the ribbon up to gather the cloak, remove the safety pin then put on the child. Pin then stitch the hem. Stitch or safety pin plastic bats or spiders to the cloak's collar, if liked.

To make the skirt, cut the net into four 50 cm (20 inch) wide strips. With the sewing machine set to the longest stitch, sew 1 cm (½ inch) in from one long edge along each piece of net. Pull up the gathering threads on each piece of net to match the child's waist measurement.

Arrange one gathered strip of net centrally over the black tape, so that the ends of the tape stick out from either side, like apron strings. Pin the net on the tape, easing the gathers into place. Repeat with the other pieces of net, arranging one on top of the other to make an 'apron' with four layers. Hand stitch in place, remove the pins then machine stitch to secure. Neaten the rough edges of the gathered net with zig-zag stitches.

Red devil

Make a red cloak in the same way as for the witch. Stitch sparkly red pompons down the front of the cloak. Team it with a red T-shirt and trousers or tights. Attach two card horns to a red knitted hat or to a head band. Disguise the face with a mask (see page 56) or face paints (see page 51).

Black cat

Combine a black leotard and tights with a black knitted hat and a cat mask (see page 56). Hand stitch on to the leotard a coloured tummy in a fabric that coordinates with the mask. Make a tail with one leg trimmed from a pair of old tights and stuffed with fabric oddments. Complete with black or white socks and gloves.

spooky masks

Whether you want a simple or sophisticated effect – for you or your child – you can make a variety of masks from fabric oddments and pieces of coloured card, or buy plain gold or silver masks from a theatrical supplier and add exotic feathers or braid.

YOU WILL NEED

heavy card or ready-made masks
ribbon, fabric and paper scraps
braid, feathers and sequins
PVA glue or glue gun
adhesive tape

Little devil

Draw an oval face shape on the back of a piece of heavy red card. Shape the oval base into a point and add horns to the top. Cut out the mask then draw a jagged mouth and oval eye shapes on the back of the mask, checking the position of eyes and mouth by measuring proportions on your child's face. Cut out facial features. Cover the back of the mouth hole with a small piece of red metallic pierced ribbon and stick in place with adhesive tape. Turn the mask over and stick on black and orange wool eyebrows. Make two small holes at the side of the mask, and thread with ribbon or elastic.

She devil

Glue tiny snipped pieces of orange lining and pink sparkly chiffon on to a ready-made gold half-face mask. You can vary the colours depending on what you have, or use coloured wrapping paper or tissue paper. Run a line of glue around the edge of the mask and press on a wide orange and red fringed braid.

Wicked witch

Use a ready-made silver half-face mask. Stick blue sequins along a line of glue above each eye radiating from the nose over the forehead. Glue black cat shapes to each cheek. Stick alternate black and blue feathers at the top of the mask.

Black cat

On a piece of paper draw a large eye mask, about 15 x 20 cm (6 x 8 inches). Curve the base to suggest cheeks and draw on ears. Cut out and use this as a template to cut out a mask from black and silver brocade or black and white fur fabric. Using the same template, cut out a piece of iron-on Vylene and press on to the back of the fabric to stiffen it. Cut a smaller eye mask from black chiffon or black iron-on Vylene and stitch or iron on to the front of the mask, if liked. Cut eye shapes from more paper, and use as a guide to cut out the eye holes, first checking the position on the child's face. Stitch four silver pipe cleaners together in the centre then stitch to a black pompon and stitch this on to the mask for a nose and whiskers. Stitch black ribbon ties or elastic to the sides of the mask.

Halloween gifts

It is easy to make your own Halloween party gifts, and fun too! Why not customize some simple cardboard boxes for your guests? Fill them with sweets or other suitable goodies for children or adults to take home with them.

Wizard wands

These no-cook sweets are ideal for children to help to make. If you don't like peppermint substitute a little orange rind instead.

YOU WILL NEED
7 g (¼ oz) dried egg white
4 tablespoons warm water
few drops of peppermint essence
500 g (1 lb) icing sugar, sifted, plus extra for rolling
green paste food colouring
16 wooden satay sticks, halved
edible coloured balls, to decorate

Put the dried egg white in a bowl and gradually mix in warm water to make a smooth thin paste. Stir in a few drops of peppermint essence and gradually stir in the icing sugar until the mixture is very stiff, mixing with your hands when it becomes too stiff to stir.

Lightly knead in a little green food colouring and roll out on a surface well dusted with icing sugar until 1 cm (½ inch) thick. Cut out 5 cm (2 inch) star shapes with a biscuit cutter and insert a halved satay stick into each. Arrange in a single layer on a tray lined with non-stick baking paper.

Press coloured balls into the stars, if liked, and leave to dry overnight. Pack in boxes lined with shredded tissue. Store up to four days.

Makes 32
Preparation time: 30 minutes
Drying time: overnight

Bags of goodies

Cut different spooky shapes from coloured cardboard. Tape each shape to a length of ribbon then tie the other end of each ribbon to a small gift wrapped in tissue paper. Put the gifts in a foil gift bag lined with squares of coloured tissue paper. Dangle some of the ribbon over the top of the bag with the tags on the end. You may like to code the tags – perhaps red devils for the men, witches' hats for the women, cats for little girls and frogs or ghosts for the boys – so that each person gets a suitable gift.

Boxing clever

STICKY SPOOKS Glue tiny Halloween confetti shapes on to small coloured cardboard gift boxes. Fill the boxes with sweets and tie the lids in place with ribbon.

TREASURE CHEST Thread coloured beads on to stiff wire and twist the ends so the beads don't unravel. Tie two strings of beads together with fine wire to make a cross shape then attach to a box lid by threading wire through two small holes in the lid. Twist the wire together and trim off the excess so the join is under the box lid. Decorate the side of the box with gold or coloured pipe cleaners stuck in place with a glue gun.

BUTTERFLY BOX Decorate the sides and lid edge of a circular cardboard gift box with gold paint – either piped straight from the tube or painted on using a small paintbrush. Leave to dry then stick on coloured sequins using a glue gun. Complete the lid of the box by attaching a butterfly Christmas tree or hat decoration to it using a glue gun.

Party games

There is no age restriction on these entertaining Halloween-themed party games, which can be real ice-breakers for all party goers with a sense of fun.

Nose on the hag

This game is a favourite with young children. Draw a witch or customize a picture of a famous person. On a separate piece of card, draw a gruesome nose with spots on. Fix a piece of double-sided tape to the back. Then blindfold a party guest and turn them around a few times to disorientate them. Then guide the guest towards the picture and see where they stick the nose. Mark the spot with a cross and note whose it is. Continue with the other guests. The person who places the nose nearest the right place on the face wins.

Murder in mind

The host chooses a 'murderer', who keeps his or her identity secret. All the participants move around the room. The murderer must wink at people to kill them, while the others must guess who is doing the killing. Those 'killed' must drop (theatrically, of course!) to the floor 'dead'. Survivors are allowed three guesses and the winner is the first one who guesses the murderer correctly.

Halloween charades

This is a game for adults or teenagers. Write the names of horror and thriller films, books and plays on to pieces of paper. Fold up and put in a bag or bowl. Divide the party guests into teams. One member of each team takes turns to pick a folded piece of paper and act out the title written on the paper. Their team mates do their best to guess what it is.

Witches' brew

Fill a bowl or 'cauldron' with items to represent body parts, such as a cauliflower for a brain, a grape for an eye, a rubber glove filled with water for a hand, linked sausages for intestines, a balloon filled with red jelly for a heart, bootlace sweets for veins. Participants sit blindfolded in a ring and as the cauldron is passed around, each pulls out an item and guesses the body part it represents.

Wizard's shopping list

This game is mainly for young children. Put a selection of Halloween items on a tray – for example a plastic spider or bat, foil-wrapped sweets, plastic fingers and a mask. Let the children look at the tray for 1 minute then, without them seeing, take away one item. The participants have to work out what it was. Repeat once or twice more.

Sweets in sugar

Hide large jelly sweets in a large shallow bowl of icing sugar. As with apple bobbing, participants have to try to pick the sweets out of the sugar using just their teeth and nothing else! Anyone who cheats and uses their hands could be given a forfeit to do. It can be messy so provide an apron for your guests!

Apple bobbing

In this traditional game apples are floated in a bowl of cold water and guests must try to take an apple out of the bowl using only their teeth. It is fun for all ages, but prepare to get wet! A preserving pan or baby bath are ideal containers. If you do this inside protect the table with a plastic cloth and some towels and provide a PVC apron for the participants. Alternatively, a drier version involves hanging cored apples on string from a door frame. Participants have to try to eat the apples with their hands tied behind their backs. The first to finish their apple is the winner.

Apple bobbing is a traditional Halloween party game.

Menu planner

Mix and match the recipes in this book to suit the kind of occasion that you have in mind, from a noisy kids' party to something more sedate for an adult gathering.

Informal supper for six adults

★ Witches' Fingers
★ Bean Pot Supper
★ Watermelon and Tequila Granita

Smart supper for six adults

★ Radicchio Salad with Blue Cheese Dressing
★ Honey-Glazed Pork
★ Maple Pumpkin Pie

Drinks and nibbles for the adults

★ Pumpkin Fondue
★ Toasted Seeds
★ Gourmet Crisps
★ Black Magic Cup
★ Ghoul's Blood

Supper for all ages

★ Pumpkin and Sage Soup
★ Honey-Glazed Pork
★ Black Cat Jelly for the kids
★ Blueberry and Port Jelly for the adults

Kids' party

★ Spider Web Pizzas
★ Witches' Fingers
★ Lantern Cakes or Wicked Witches
★ Black Cat Jelly

Bonfire treats

★ Pumpkin and Sage Soup served in mugs
★ Spider Web Pizzas
★ Spooky Cookies
★ Cinnamon and Pumpkin Muffins

Get set

Add a little sophistication and glamour to your table (see right). Keep the plastic Halloween novelties for the kids and dress the table with a coloured orange runner, or cheat and make your own with some luxurious folded fabric. Add small pumpkin lanterns for eye-catching shafts of light that twinkle over Halloween-themed foil confetti. Pumpkin place cards indicate where guests should sit, but could also contain a spooky rhyme or adult game to use as an ice-breaker.

Index

Acknowledgements

Executive Editor SARAH FORD
Editor SHARON ASHMAN
Design Manager TOKIKO MORISHIMA
Designer LISA TAI
Senior Production Controller JO SIM
Food and Craft Stylist SARA LEWIS
Stylist CLARE HUNT
Photographer DAVID JORDAN
Illustrations LINE + LINE

All photography Octopus Publishing
Group Limited/David Jordan except
for the following:

Octopus Publishing Group
Limited/Philip Webb 24
Clive Nichols/Designer: Clare
Matthews 5, 15, 61